WELSH STEAM

WELSH STEAM

RAILWAY PHOTOGRAPHS AT THE NATIONAL LIBRARY OF WALES

Gwyn Briwnant-Jones

CARDIFF
UNIVERSITY OF WALES PRESS
NATIONAL LIBRARY OF WALES

1991

British Library Cataloguing in Publication Data
Briwnant-Jones, Gwyn, *1932–*
    Welsh steam: railway photographs at the National
Library of Wales.
    I. Title
    385.09429
ISBN 0–7083–1114–8

Jacket design by Design Principle, Cardiff
Typeset by BP Integraphics, Bath
Printed in Great Britain by The Bath Press, Bath

CONTENTS

ACKNOWLEDGEMENTS

I wish to record my appreciation of the help given so readily by Dr D. Huw Owen and all the staff of the National Library, particularly the staff of the photographic unit, whose expertise has ensured optimum results from so many negatives of varying quality.

My sincere thanks are also extended to Michael Scott Archer, Revd F. A. Cliff and Glyn Owen (Corwen) for allowing the National Library staff to copy original prints in their private collections.

G. Briwnant-Jones.   Llangollen
                                                                     February 1991.

ABBREVIATIONS

AD & R	Alexandra Docks & Railway Co.
CHR	Chester & Holyhead Railway
GWR	Great Western Railway
LNWR	London North Western Railway
M & M	Manchester & Milford Railway
NLW	National Library of Wales, Aberystwyth
PC & N	Pontypridd, Caerphilly & Newport Junction
P & TR	Pembroke & Tenby Railway
PTR	Port Talbot Railway, frequently used form of PTD & R
SWR	South Wales Railway

Abbreviations used to identify sources within the National Library of Wales are listed here according to collection. All material in this volume is held in the collections of the National Library of Wales, Aberystwyth.

AJL	A. J. Lewis, Aberystwyth
DCH	D. C. Harries, Llandeilo
GC	Geoff Charles
GO	Glyn Owen, Corwen
JT	John Thomas
Lett	Lettsome (Photographer), Llangollen
MSA	Michael Scott Archer
PPC	Picture postcards at NLW
PTD & R	Port Talbot Docks & Railway
TWJ	Thomas W. Jones, Tregaron
WDJ	W. D. Johns, Cardiff

RAILWAY PHOTOGRAPHS AT THE
NATIONAL LIBRARY OF WALES

The Department of Pictures and Maps at the National Library of Wales at Aberystwyth is the depository of a vast quantity of graphic and printed material relating to many aspects of Welsh life, railways included. As yet, no index system exists to facilitate access to the railway material in a single operation; it is therefore not possible, at present, to claim knowledge of each and every rail-related image in the Library's vast collection, although all the familiar prints which may already have graced the pages of various publications have come readily to hand.

In addition to the prints which were anticipated within the collection, the greatest pleasure, undoubtedly, has been the occasional 'discovery' of the unexpected. First sight of the print of the 1911 Royal Train at Aber-miwl (Abermule) provides such an example. This previously little-known image is the work of an amateur cameraman, J. D. K. Lloyd, who not only took a 'snap-shot' of the Special passing through Aber-miwl but, of equal significance to the historian perhaps, also appears to have used his 'waiting time' profitably by recording the more humble Kerry branch train standing alongside the nearby platform. Another instance was when the full significance began to dawn of what appeared initially to be yet another manufacturer's photograph — the portrait of a Sharp Stewart 2–4–0 passenger engine. This is particularly worthy of note as it ranks amongst the earliest railway prints in the Library's collection. It was produced for the manufacturer in 1861 and depicts what was, supposedly, a locomotive of the emerging Oswestry & Newtown Railway. The presence of the print amongst the Glansevern Papers of the Humphreys Owen family presents something of a mystery, even allowing for the fact that the family were supporters of the early Montgomeryshire railways. Differences in detail suggest that the locomotive of the historic photograph did not, in fact, grace the rails of mid Wales, although it bore a strong resemblance to the little 2–4–0s which were later operated by the Cambrian Railways.

Perhaps the most important photographic collections within the Library, however, are those of John Thomas, who practised during the last three decades of the nineteenth century, and Geoff Charles, a newspaper photographer/journalist who was most active from 1939 to 1970. Although separated by some four decades, both men produced comprehensive portrayals of many aspects of Welsh life, including various railway topics.

Both Thomas and Charles travelled extensively throughout the country,

1

yet they confined most of their photographic activity to north and mid Wales. This restricted field of operation represents a considerable loss as far as the recording of railway life in the south is concerned.

Thomas initially spent much of his time photographing ministers of religion, apparently a most lucrative venture; these, together with his portraits of more humble folk at work or in repose, proved to be the financial mainstay of his enterprise for many years. He commenced in 1867 at a religious convention in Llanidloes and soon became adept at arranging and photographing a variety of groups, provided they appeared to have commercial potential. He frequently visited the harbours and quarries of the north and usually photographed groups of men during their lunch hour, when the light was usually at its best and he was least likely to incur the displeasure of the management. Although born in Cardiganshire, Thomas lived in and operated his business from Liverpool. He toured Wales each summer for over thirty years, travelling in a horse-drawn van which could provide makeshift overnight accommodation, although its prime purpose was to serve as a mobile darkroom, as all the early plates were developed by the collodion, or 'wet', process and had to be processed within fifteen minutes of the exposure being made. Thomas amassed a unique record of Welsh life during the latter decades of the nineteenth century and at the behest of O. M. Edwards, publisher of the Welsh magazine *Cymru*, he selected and sold 'at a reasonable price' 3,000 glass negatives which represented a cross-section of his best work. These were later donated by Sir Ifan ab Owen Edwards to the National Library in 1927. Tragically, none of Thomas's remaining negatives, estimated at over 17,000 in number, are thought to exist today and, although comparatively few can have held much railway interest, the example of the print of the Crewe locomotive at Llanybydder provides some indication of what may have been lost. Sadly, Thomas died in 1905 before he had time to compile notes to accompany the 3,000 surviving plates: the vast majority are not even dated.

In marked contrast, the Geoff Charles collection has been carefully preserved in its entirety and all relevant dates and other details are now stored on computer disks. Whereas the equipment and techniques of the two men obviously differed greatly they were, in essence, doing much the same kind of work; both reveal great affection and respect for their subjects and both must surely have had more than a passing interest in railways.

All the photographs are here presented according to geographic areas, which roughly correspond to the current county structure, in an attempt to introduce a degree of cohesion to what is otherwise a rather unrelated collection of prints. Although the National Library seeks to offer equal representation of all Welsh interests, the collection of railway material does not, regrettably, fully portray the history and development of rail transport in Wales.

This factor has resulted in an unavoidable imbalance in the content of the album. The poor representation of the London North Western Railway and its successors in both north and south Wales, for example, is particularly surprising and much regretted, although the limited presence in the collection of the Great Central and Midland Railways is not entirely unexpected for these companies were less prominent west of Offa's Dyke. However, the almost total absence of prints of the various south Wales valley lines in pre-grouping days represents a most surprising omission and constitutes one of the major disappointments encountered during compilation. Only one album of photographs of the Port Talbot Docks & Railway Company attempts to correct this imbalance and, until the recent discovery of the W. D. Johns collection, the writer was unaware of any other south Wales valley scenes in the National Library collection, outside the files of picture postcards. The rich railway heritage of Gwent is conspicuous by its almost total absence.

Understandably, therefore, the areas best represented are those of mid and north Wales, where both narrow- and standard-gauge lines feature prominently. As may perhaps be anticipated, the Aberystwyth area itself is well covered, particularly by A. J. Lewis.

It might here be noted that the difference between the quality of an original print, or a print from an original negative, and its published form has to be experienced at first hand for the variation to be appreciated fully. This is especially the case when prints are made from some of the early glass negatives or from some of the more modern 5cm × 4cm negatives: both are capable of yielding extremely fine prints when carefully exposed and processed.

With the notable exception of the Geoff Charles collection and certain individual prints which are acknowledged elsewhere, it would seem that few railway-biased additions have been made to the Library's collection in recent times. The National Library of Wales wishes to maintain its proud record of safeguarding photographic collections for future generations. Therefore, considering the enormous interest in railway photography, particularly during the last quarter century, the Library would be very pleased to receive details of relevant items and collections, especially from those who have obviously derived great pleasure from photographing, or collecting photographs of, Welsh railways.

RAILWAYS IN WALES

With the exception of isolated sections of early feeder tramways, usually connecting industrial sites with canal or sea transport, railways did not emerge as a means of transport within Wales until the 1840–5 period, when the need for improved services between London and Ireland became apparent. The routes finally chosen, along the northern coast from Chester to Holyhead and Dublin (Chester & Holyhead Railway, incorporated 1844), and the southern route from Gloucester to west Wales and Cork (South Wales Railway, incorporated 1845), still serve the same purpose to this day, although the latter route has been modified somewhat over the years. The opening of the tunnel under the Severn in 1886 obviated the detour via Gloucester, the later development of Fishguard (1906) at the expense of New Milford (Neyland), and the construction of the Swansea 'cut-off' line just before the First World War all contributed to an improved service to southern Ireland.

The industries which were established along the valleys of both north and south Wales spawned short, independent lines which superseded most of the early tramways; those in the south conveyed vast tonnages of coal annually from pits to docks, whilst the branch lines of the north were tailored mainly to the needs of the slate industry and in some instances led logically to the extension and development of existing and often vast tramway systems within the quarries themselves. The narrow-gauge concept (usually between 1ft 11 ½ in. and 2ft 3in.) offered several advantages over the standard gauge, principally the comparative ease of construction and economy of operation and, in particular, the elimination of the uneconomic transhipment from internal quarry wagons to standard-gauge wagons for the comparatively short journey to the coast. Thus were born the narrow-gauge systems of the north and the heavily constructed standard-gauge branch-lines of the south. The colourful narrow-gauge lines were quick to exploit the majestic scenery through which they ran, and were much loved and patronized by summer tourists. The lines of the south, in contrast, were in no position to attract tourists; indeed, most passengers were decidedly secondary to the serious business of moving truly gargantuan tonnages of coal, iron and steel. For this reason, perhaps, the branch-lines of the industrial south were mistakenly perceived for many years as bleak and boring concerns — a misconception which has survived until comparatively recent times.

The apparent polarization of early Welsh railway development thus created an enormous void in the central regions of Wales which remained until the 1850s. The lack of any major industry in these areas together with the sparse population ensured that financial speculators were not easily attracted, although a plethora of schemes had been advanced from as early as 1836. Notable amongst these was a Gloucester–New Quay scheme and a projection by Charles Vignoles for a line from Shrewsbury via Llangollen and Barmouth to Porth Dinllaen, on the northern coast of the Llŷn peninsula. There were many others, but perhaps the most famous was the proposal for an extension of the Great Western Railway's Paddington–Worcester line, also to Porth Dinllaen. Planned by no less an engineer than Isambard Kingdom Brunel, this line was projected via Ludlow, Montgomery, Newtown, Talerddig, Dinas Mawddwy and Barmouth, and would have been built to the broad gauge of 7ft. The considerable amount of heavy engineering required, together with the Gauge Commissioners' report of 1846 recommending no further increase of broad-gauge territory, were sufficient to defeat the proposal. A line across mid Wales, on an east–west axis, was only provided by the promotion of a series of short, local lines which eventually amalgamated under the banner of the Cambrian Railways in 1864.

Various other cross-country routes, such as Ruabon–Dolgellau, Afon-wen–Caernarfon, Rhyl–Corwen, Aberystwyth–Carmarthen and Moat Lane–Brecon completed a basic network which was to serve Wales for the better part of a century, until ruthlessly dismembered during the mid 1960s by Dr Beeching. Inadequate consideration was then given to modernizing and adapting the service within necessary financial constraints and no thought was given to producing a cohesive transport structure, nor consideration afforded to possible requirements of transport in the future. Some judicious rationalization was obviously required to adapt what was a Victorian network to the needs of the latter half of the twentieth century but the easy, short-term option was taken and vast proportions of the country's rich transport heritage were jettisoned with a short-sightedness which has become increasingly apparent in more recent times.

Ironically, the majority of the railways of Wales were in better order during the early 1960s than at any time in the previous twenty years. The deprivations of the war period had been rectified: hundreds of miles of permanent way had been re-laid: stations were repaired and repainted; signalling was modernized and new rolling stock introduced. It was unfortunate that this period of recovery coincided with increasing use of the private motor car. The railways, which had been under state control since 1940 and state ownership since 1948, failed to compete. The principal remedies appeared to be cut-backs and increased fares. When these elements were combined with high expenditure on track and engineering, the formula could lead only to contraction and eventual closure; country branch-lines were amongst the first to suffer.

This has, of necessity, been the merest outline of the development of railways in Wales. Detailed accounts are available of almost every Welsh line, and a short list of books for further reading is given in the Bibliography.

6

Irish Mail Routes

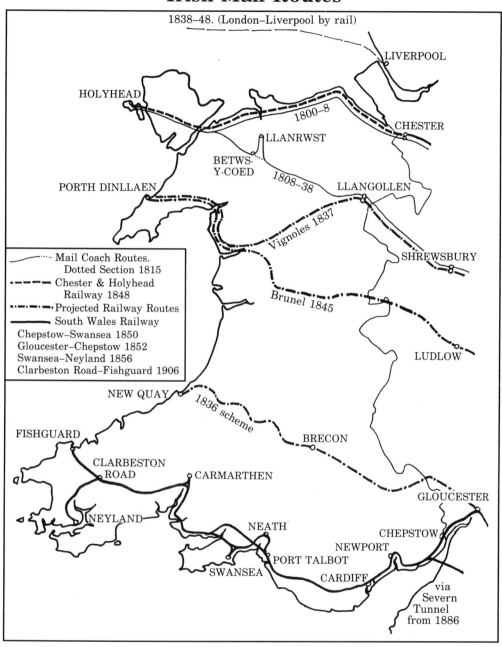

1838–48. (London–Liverpool by rail)

LIVERPOOL

HOLYHEAD

CHESTER

1800–8

LLANRWST

BETWS-Y-COED

1808–38

LLANGOLLEN

PORTH DINLLAEN

Vignoles 1837

SHREWSBURY

—····· Mail Coach Routes.
　　　　Dotted Section 1815
— — — Chester & Holyhead
　　　　Railway 1848
—·—·—· Projected Railway Routes
———— South Wales Railway
Chepstow–Swansea 1850
Gloucester–Chepstow 1852
Swansea–Neyland 1856
Clarbeston Road–Fishguard 1906

Brunel 1845

LUDLOW

NEW QUAY

1836 scheme

BRECON

FISHGUARD

CLARBESTON
ROAD

CARMARTHEN

GLOUCESTER

NEYLAND

NEATH

CHEPSTOW

NEWPORT

PORT TALBOT

SWANSEA

CARDIFF

via
Severn
Tunnel
from 1886

1   NORTH-WEST WALES

Although narrow-gauge tramways existed in north-west Wales from as early as 1801 (Penrhyn Quarry railway) and 1828 (Nantlle Tramway), the first standard-gauge main-line was the Irish Mail route from Chester to Holyhead, which was completed in 1850 with the opening of the bridge across the Menai Straits. The engineer was the celebrated Robert Stephenson; his new line reduced the journey time between London and Holyhead to just over nine and a half hours.

With the exception of the path chosen directly across Anglesey, Stephenson followed the almost level although sometimes restricted course along the coastal strip from Chester. The modest population along this route at the time of the line's construction changed markedly when improved social and working conditions in nearby Lancashire ensured a dramatic increase during the summer months as the industrial workers of the north enjoyed the luxury of annual holidays and discovered the ease with which the railway could convey them to the new and expanding coastal resorts.

The possibilities for large-scale exploitation of the region's mineral wealth were confined largely to the quarrying of slate, but the existence of established tramway systems for the short journeys to the seaboard ensured minimal development of the standard-gauge rail network.

Only a handful of branch-lines were built, particularly in comparison with the number of lines constructed elsewhere in Wales for the transportation of coal and other heavy commodities. Most have now closed but the Llandudno–Llandudno Junction and Blaenau Ffestiniog–Llandudno Junction branches remain open for passenger operation, the latter also being used for the periodic removal of atomic waste from the Trawsfynydd nuclear power station to Sellafield, via the surviving portion of the old Great Western Bala Junction–Blaenau Ffestiniog branch and the 1964 connecting link at Blaenau. The remaining standard-gauge survivor is the Gaerwen–Amlwch branch in Anglesey, now retained as a freight-only line.

Perhaps the most regrettable of the branch-line closures in north-west Wales was the line from Bangor to Afon-wen. It used to link the north Wales and Cardigan Bay sea coasts and its closure deprived the country of one of the very few through routes on a north–south axis.

North-West Wales

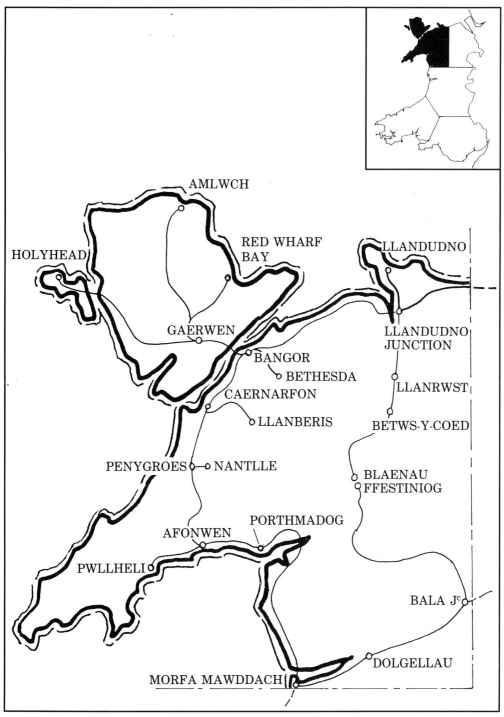

1.

2.

3

1. Rather surprisingly, the NLW Collection contains fewer images of the London North Western Railway harbour at Holyhead than might be expected, despite its being considered the main port for the bulk of the Irish traffic. Nevertheless, this view includes the Custom House, the replica of the doric arch at Euston, and the Irish Mail boat. *c.* 1930.] [PPC.

2. Conwy Castle and town walls (Chester & Holyhead Railway). Foreground railway interest, including the commodious goods shed, whitewashed cattle wagons, signal box and the twin portals of Stephenson's tubular bridge over the Conwy, is balanced by an intriguing glimpse of the comparatively undeveloped area around Llandudno Junction, just discernible across the estuary. *c.* 1895.] [JT Coll.

3. Few photographs exist of railway construction in Wales although the completion of an impressive masonry viaduct on the LNWR Llandudno Junction–Blaenau Ffestiniog branch was well recorded by John Thomas. Work commenced near Betws-y-coed on the construction of Pont Tan-yr-allt, or Pont Cethin as it is known locally, in August 1875; it was completed by August 1878. According to a note to the photographer from the contractors, the structure comprises seven visible arches and a further thirty-one which are obscured. The viaduct is six yards wide and almost a quarter of a mile in length. The largest dimension of any stone used in its construction is 20ft and the heaviest weighs 7½ tons. The thirty-one chambers of the enclosed arches are interconnected and were used by the navvies as lodging quarters during the construction of the line. The contractors were Owen Jones of Glasgwm Hall, and O. Gethin Jones of Penmachno, who is probably the figure portrayed above the centre arch. *c.* 1878.] [JT Coll.

4.

5.

4. The interchange sidings at Nantlle, where the branch engine, a LNWR 0–6–2T, has drawn its short train of four-wheel stock forward onto the locomotive turntable. This special manœuvre, together with the adjacent grouping of the narrow-gauge slate wagons, was probably for the photographer's benefit.
   c. 1885.]   [JT Coll.

5. Pen-y-groes, on the LNWR Caernarfon–Afon-wen line, was the junction for the short 1½-mile branch to Nantlle. A convenient LNWR 0–6–0 is commandeered as a stage prop, whilst Thomas practises his proven formula for selling prints, although it would be interesting to learn how many of the twenty-eight in the group returned firm orders.
   The station buildings changed little during almost a century of operation.
   c. 1885.]   [JT Coll.

6. Ysgol Glan-y-pwll, Ffestiniog, dominates this view of four early private-owner wagons. With the exception of the canvas-covered wagon on the left, all are fitted with 'dumb buffers', that is, solid buffers formed by an extension of the solebars, as opposed to the later, sprung variety. The first open wagon, from the left, claims the added distinction of four unusual cast metal plates, declaring its number and owner: wagon no. 1154, belonging to Richard Evans & Co., and working from Haydock Colliery, near St Helens.
   The presence of the disc signal, behind the grounded horse-box, indicates the location of the Ffestiniog Railway, at a lower level and out of sight of the camera.
   c. 1875.]   [JT Coll.

6.

7.

7. A small family group poses informally at Minffordd station of the Cambrian Railways, as former Oswestry & Newtown Railway 0–6–0 No. 19, *Hercules*, and crew take advantage of the photographer's presence to create a brief interlude whilst shunting the nearby exchange sidings. Large quantities of slate were trans-shipped here from the narrow-gauge Festiniog Railway between 1867 and 1946.

   The photographer neglected to note the date of this occasion but *Hercules*, built in 1862, lost its name-plates, along with the rest of the class, during the 1886–91 period.
   c. 1885.]   [MSA Coll.

8. Penrhyndeudraeth station during the 1880s. The two-way slotted signal, operated not
from the comfort of a snug signal cabin but from levers placed in the open at the foot of the
post, the low platform and the rather irregular trackwork were hallmarks of the Cambrian
during this period. Poor standards of maintenance, reflected by the worn paintwork and
weather-beaten stucco walls, provide further evidence of the tight financial constraints
which affected the line during the whole of its existence.

[JT Coll.

9.

9. Until the Beeching era, the volume of parcels traffic handled by the railways was truly phenomenal but reductions of the network and facilities during the 1960s prevented the railways from continuing such a comprehensive service. At the period of this photograph, goods as diverse as cigarettes, saucepans and motor-car accessories continued to come by rail and the Goodyear Company still wrapped their spare tyres, partly visible amongst the parcels being loaded onto the Blaenau Ffestiniog train at Llandudno Junction on 16 January 1964.

[GC Coll.

10. Although diesel power was introduced on a vast scale as the principal replacement for
steam propulsion during the mid 1960s, other aspects of railway operation were not
modernized at that time, which helped to create many anachronisms. The driver of a
twentieth-century diesel train exchanges nineteenth-century signalling tokens on the
Llandudno Junction–Blaenau Ffestiniog branch on 16 January 1964.

[GC Coll.

11.

11. Heralds of sad tidings. Station staff at Porthaethwy (Menai Bridge), the junction on the
Chester & Holyhead Railway for the Caernarfon and Afon-wen line, paste up notice of
withdrawal of passenger services on 1 January 1966. Peeling paintwork reveals the
manner in which this particular building was neglected during the final years.

[GC Coll.

12. Interior view of the former Great Western Booking Office at Blaenau Ffestiniog on 7 January 1960, as one of the final tickets is issued after being punched on the old Edmondson machine.

On such occasions, a few mementoes such as old tickets, fare-charts or impedimenta bearing the magic initials 'G.W.R.' might find their way into a private collection, but the bulk of redundant paperwork and artefacts was placed unceremoniously on a bonfire or the waste-tip. Over the years much of interest, and occasionally of historical value, has been unwittingly discarded.

Edmondson tickets survived in use on British Rail until February 1990, when the last tickets were issued at Pembrey in Dyfed, terminating a system which had served the railways of Britain for 150 years.

[GC Coll.

13.

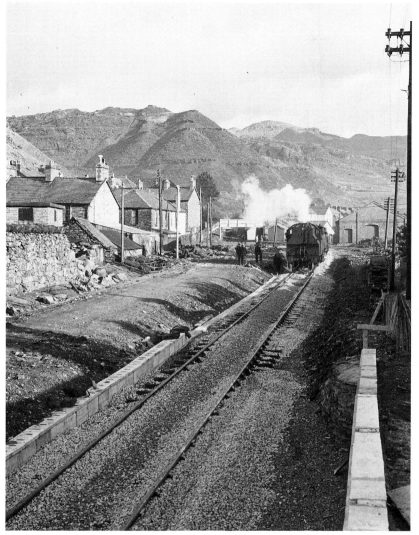

13. The new alignment at Blaenau Ffestiniog, looking toward the GWR station. The standard and narrow-gauge openings in the goods shed are easily discerned in this view which shows an Ivatt Class 2 2–6–2T, one of the few steam locomotives to traverse the link-line, in charge of the ballast train. The connection was opened on 20 April 1964. The remains of the line to the Ffestiniog's former terminus at Duffws, passing beneath the light-coloured bridge in the centre of the picture, are just visible. Slate tips of the Votty (*sic*) and Bowydd Quarry provide a prominent background.
1 January 1964.]   [GC Coll.

14. A typical John Thomas masterpiece. All the necessary ingredients were organized by the photographer, and no one seemed to mind if the service train was delayed whilst the Permanent Way trolley was trundled into position and Thomas 'stage-managed' the station staff: the result certainly seemed to justify the means.
Trawsfynydd *c.* 1900.]   [JT Coll.

(Overleaf)

15. Beeching had decided to close the Ruabon–Barmouth Junction line on 18 January 1965, but severe flooding on 12 December 1964 undermined the track-bed near Llandderfel, resulting in an abrupt and unscheduled end to through services. Merioneth County Council stipulated that the track for most of the route should remain *in situ*, with a view to possible reopening, but the preservation of standard-gauge lines was then in its infancy and the opportunity was lost.
c. 1966.]   [GC Coll.

16. The rails were removed from the Ruabon line at Barmouth Junction, latterly called Morfa Mawddach, on 2 April 1969; Machynlleth-based D5045 provided the motive power on this occasion.
[GC Coll.

15.

16.

17. Few sights are more depressing than locations of commerce and industry in a state of decay. Dolgellau may not have been a particularly prominent railway centre but, from 1869, it was a junction between the Cambrian and Great Western railways. The only evidence of this function remaining when demolition took place, a century later, was the old turntable pit near the signal-box. So many branch-line closures and wholesale scrapping of surplus equipment took place in the 1960s and early 1970s that most contracts were awarded to private contractors: British Rail was ill-equipped to deal with demolition on such a vast scale. The site of the joint station and the track-bed is now occupied by the Dolgellau bypass.
11 January 1969.]   [GC Coll.

2 NORTH-EAST WALES

Two lines linked the eastern and western regions of north Wales; the gently graded Irish Mail route along the coast between Chester and Holyhead, and the more difficult secondary line which threaded the mountains further south, from Ruabon to Dolgellau and the coast of Cardigan Bay at Barmouth.

The principal connections between these east–west routes were provided by the former Shrewsbury & Chester Railway (later the Great Western Company), which opened in 1848 and ran through the Welsh Border country, and a second north–south line further west, which linked Rhyl and Corwen by means of the Vale of Clwyd and Denbigh, Ruthin & Corwen railways, later operated by the London & North Western and the London Midland & Scottish companies.

Unlike their counterparts in the slate regions of Gwynedd, the branch-lines of the north-east were, with but few exceptions, built for the conveyance of coal, iron and steel, and were located principally in the Ruabon–Wrexham area.

With the engineering of the Chester & Holyhead line entrusted to Stephenson, the planning of the Shrewsbury–Chester and the Ruabon--Dolgellau lines was contracted to a young Scot who had settled in north-east Wales. The figure of Henry Robertson is generally much neglected in the annals of Welsh railway history, but his achievements rank alongside those of his more illustrious contemporary. He was given the task of reconstructing one of Stephenson's bridges (over the Dee near Chester), which had collapsed in May 1847, but Robertson's most enduring monuments, undoubtedly, are located in the Ruabon– Chirk region, where his 1,508 feet-long and 147 feet-high viaduct over the Dee and the slightly smaller but still impressive structure over the River Ceiriog at Chirk are both still in daily use by the Chester–Shrewsbury services of British Rail.

Among other secondary lines in the area which operated passenger services were the Mold Railway, from Saltney Ferry Junction to Denbigh, and the railways which formed an end-on junction at Wrexham Central station, the Wrexham, Mold & Connah's Quay line — later operated by the Great Central and the London & North Eastern railways (the only incursion by these companies into Wales) — and the Wrexham, Ellesmere & Whitchurch Railway, which formed part of the Cambrian system.

The only passenger services currently operated by British Rail in this area are those along the north Wales coast; from Shrewsbury to Chester, and from Wrexham Central to Bidston, on the Wirral.

North-East Wales

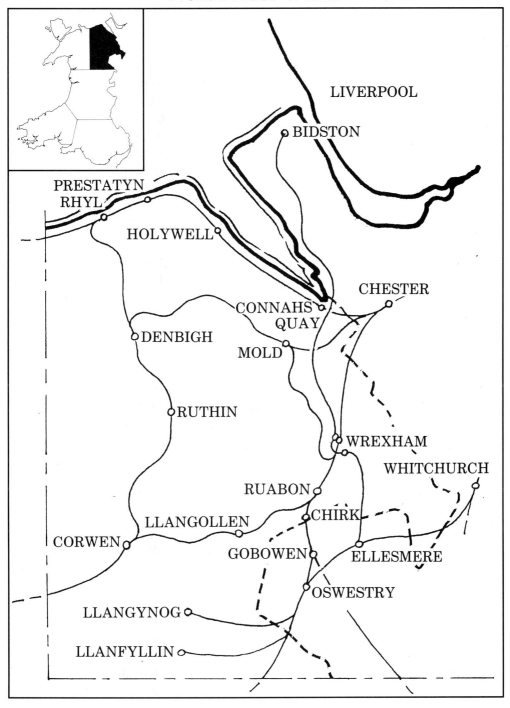

LIVERPOOL

BIDSTON

PRESTATYN
RHYL
HOLYWELL

CHESTER

CONNAHS
QUAY

DENBIGH

MOLD

RUTHIN

WREXHAM

WHITCHURCH

RUABON

LLANGOLLEN

CHIRK

CORWEN

GOBOWEN

ELLESMERE

OSWESTRY

LLANGYNOG

LLANFYLLIN

18.

19.

18. Llangollen station (I), and the old, narrow road bridge across the Dee, with its irregular arches and darker stonework indicating its original height, before Henry Robertson's plans for the railway necessitated the raising of the road to clear the tracks.

    One tall slotted signal, just discernible beneath the crenellated *Siamber Wen* and bridge tower in the centre of the picture, was considered sufficient to safeguard railway operations. The platform canopy, footbridge to the 'down' side, and the signal box, had yet to be built.
    Late 1880s.] [JT Coll.

19. Llangollen station (II). The recently installed signal and signal-box, resplendent in fresh topcoat, and just visible behind the new Wolverhampton-built member of the 2021 class of 0-6-0ST, provide the backcloth for a crowd of shunters, platform staff and engineering workers. The presence of the latter and the indication that the lower edge of the station roof has received attention suggest that work had commenced on the provision of the platform awning and footbridge to the 'down' side.
    c. 1905.] [Lett: MSA Coll.

20. 0-4-0ST No. 45 was constructed by the Great Western Railway at their Stafford Road works in Wolverhampton, to replace an old four-coupled shunting engine of the former Shrewsbury & Birmingham Railway, in June 1880. It was the only 0-4-0ST of conventional design to be built at a GWR works, and always worked in the north, mainly from Croes Newydd. It achieved a modest mileage of only 430,000 before being withdrawn in April 1938 from Croes Newydd, where it was photographed shortly before the end.
    [GC Coll.

21.

22.

21. During the heyday of steam, Corwen Station boasted a bookstall and a Refreshment Room run by a private contractor, J. W. Plack, who produced special crockery bearing his name and the name of the station. Such an item, should it have survived, would be prized by today's collectors of railwayana!

   The photographer who recorded this tranquil scene was the Llangollen-based Mr Lettsome: he sold picture postcards of this view, but the original glass plate, together with the bulk of his excellent work, has long since disappeared.
   c. 1910.]   [GO Coll.

22. Flooding along the valley of the Dee was a regular occurrence before construction of the Flood Prevention Control at Bala in the 1950s. This picture postcard shows Corwen's seldom photographed engine shed, the coal-stage, the turntable and the main line to Bala (in front of the signal box) under water.
   c. 1910.]   [GO Coll.

23. At one time, the busing of schoolchildren was almost unknown in Wales, although the 'train-ing' of day scholars was regular practice. From Drws-y-nant to Dolgellau and thence to Barmouth, from Carno to Newtown, Borth to Machynlleth, Brynaman to Ammanford, Caerffili and Bargoed to Pengam, and in countless similar situations throughout the length and breadth of Wales, pupils arrived for and departed from their daily dose of erudition via the railway.

   On 5 February 1959, Corwen's lively young hopefuls return home from Bala at the end of a hard and active day.

                                                                                    [GC Coll.

24.

25.

24. An expectant crowd of well-wishers and officials assemble at Llangollen station to greet the first overseas competitors for the inaugural International Eisteddfod in July 1947. The festival's originator and Musical Director for the first thirty years, W. S. Gwynne Williams, is visible in the lower right-hand corner, whilst the bespectacled official facing the camera, in the centre of the picture, is Gwilym Bethel, for many years also associated with the Lewis Eisteddfod in Liverpool.
July 1947.]   [GC Coll.

25. The approaching Gobowen–Oswestry auto train, propelled by a small locomotive obscured by the single coach, was about to swing to the track diverging to its right when the photographer recorded this scene at Oswestry in 1950. The line from Gobowen was a Great Western line; the Cambrian main-line, to Whitchurch, went to the right of the signal-box. The shunting locomotive, built for the Cambrian by Beyer Peacock in pre-grouping days, was one of only ten survivors when the photograph was taken; the class had all disappeared by 1954. Virtually all that remains of this scene today is the footbridge which once spanned the tracks.

[GC Coll.

26. Footplate crews supplied their own food during long periods at work: no comfortable, subsidized works canteen for them! Fireman Geoff Williams, of Moss Lane, hands an empty food-box to driver Vernon Jones, on completion of their turn of duty at Wrexham in June 1953.   [GC Coll.

26.

27.

28.

27. Former Great Western Railway 4–4–0 No. 9010 approaches a handsome bracket signal at Oswestry, with a train from Welshpool, in June 1956.

[GC Coll.

28. The fireman, Ken Jones, protects a road crossing at Porthywaen as Dean Goods 0–6–0 No. 2449 works the last train over the Llangynog–Llanrhaeadr branch, in east Montgomeryshire, on Monday, 30 June 1952.

[GC Coll.

29. Guard A. Davies, fireman Ken Jones and driver John Hughes pose on the footplate of the 60-year old Dean veteran during the last journey.
30 June 1952.] [GC Coll.

30.

30. In the past, most small boys yearned, at one time or another, to climb onto the footplate of a
live steam engine. Comparatively few were granted the privilege, but the photographer's
son was fortunate; he was shown the mysteries of some of the controls by an indulgent
crew, at Oswestry.
1 January 1950.]   [GC Coll.

31. Some locomotives had the knack of capturing the limelight more frequently than the
remainder of their class; GW 4–4–0 No. 9017 was such an example. It features in many
photographs of the old Cambrian lines and is the only example of its class to have survived
into the preservation era.

On 31 December 1947, it hauled the last Great Western train from Oswestry to
Aberystwyth. The former administrative headquarters of the old Cambrian Railways
Company at Oswestry, behind the locomotive in this photograph, is now a Grade II Listed
building which currently serves a most menial role as a DIY store.

[GC Coll.

31.

3 MID WALES

Compared with the major trunk routes across north and south Wales, the remainder of the country's through routes were constructed in piecemeal, almost haphazard, fashion by linking together a series of short, local schemes. Few lines had the financial strength to exceed a length of thirty miles; the majority were considerably shorter. They existed on meagre traffic and survived only as the result of amalgamation, either amongst themselves or with one of the larger English companies which were always ready to offer support, even though they frequently appeared more concerned with keeping rivals at bay than developing the sparse local traffic.

The early schemes were grandiose but the financial resources were pitiful in comparison, and were it not for the philanthropic approach of some of Wales's own engineers and contractors, there is little doubt that most of the more mountainous regions of Wales, from Rhyl to Brecon, would hardly have seen a railway at all.

Amongst the Welshmen who devoted their energies, expertise or resources to this end was Benjamin Piercy, the engineer from Trefeglwys. He commenced as assistant to Robertson but later planned a great many of the schemes for mid and north Wales. David Davies, the famous contractor and entrepreneur from Llandinam, the archetypal self-made man of Victorian Wales, was another key figure and, in many respects, one of the most important Welshmen of his period. Finally, Thomas Savin, a one-time mercer from Oswestry, changed the course of his life when, at thirty years of age, he took to railway contracting on a most ambitious and adventurous scale.

The three men actually worked as a team for a short while but they eventually parted company. Piercy remained a railway engineer and his work took him to Sardinia, along with Davies; David Davies, however, eventually made his greatest mark in south Wales, extracting coal from the upper reaches of the Rhondda and exporting it along his own railway and through his own dock at Barry.

Thomas Savin was possibly, in some respects, the most exciting member of the trio. His star ascended with increasing brilliance over the mid Wales railway scene from 1856 but within a decade his enthusiasm, energy and keen business acumen had contributed to his own downfall. Lacking Davies's natural caution, Savin's brasher approach and tendency to be involved simultaneously with too many inadequately financed schemes, together with his propensity for accepting vast numbers of shares in lieu of payment, inevitably led to his downfall. He became bankrupt in February 1866, yet, without his energy and forbearance and the generosity and goodwill of David Davies, the majority of the railways of mid Wales might never have been constructed.

By 1865, the Aberystwyth & Welsh Coast Railway had joined the original constituents of the Cambrian Railways, namely the Llanidloes & Newtown Railway, the Oswestry & Newtown Railway, the Newtown & Machynlleth Railway, and the Oswestry, Ellesmere & Whitchurch Railway. They were joined by the Mid-Wales Company in 1904 and remained to become part of the Great Western Railway in 1922.

Mid Wales

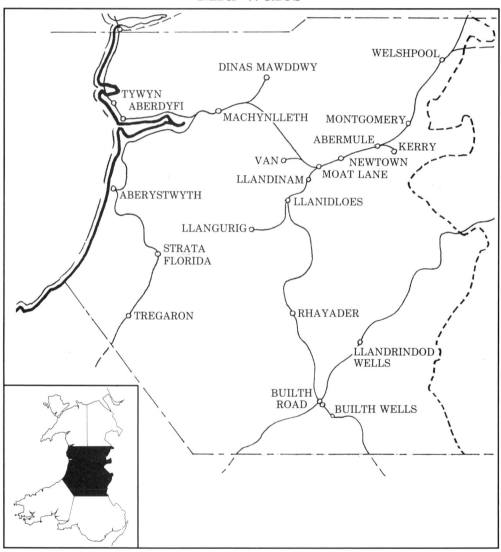

32. The theory has been advanced that this photograph may, perhaps, have been supplied to Mrs Anne Warburton Owen as a pattern for an engraving on a bugle which she presented to the Third Montgomeryshire Railway Rifles in 1861. There is also the possibility that it was given to Mrs Owen merely as an example of the type of locomotive expected on the Oswestry & Newtown Railway, for it is not unlikely that the redoubtable Mrs Owen may well have sought some reassurance of the outward appearance of the new steam monsters before she sanctioned their appearance within two miles of her home at Glansevern, near Berriew.
1861.]   [Sharp Stewart Official.

(Overleaf)
33. Some of the earliest Board meetings of the Cambrian Company were held at Welshpool station, an elegant building more akin to a French château than a rural Welsh railway station. At the outset, considerable pressure was exerted for the main workshops of the company to be established at Welshpool, in many ways the obvious location, but strong representations from Oswestry proved successful and the headquarters of this most Welsh of railways was established just across the Welsh–English border, in Shropshire.
c. 1905.]   [PPC.

34. Montgomery station *c.* 1890; a delightful view of a country station which still appeals although it has been used in several publications. The Cambrian's tall two-arm slotted signal is prominent, as is the down train headed by a 2–4–0, believed to be No. 53, formerly named *Gladstone*.

[JT Coll.

33.

RAILWAY STATION WELSHPOOL

34.

35. King George V, Queen Mary and Prince Edward travelled extensively in the United Kingdom following the coronation ceremony at Westminster Abbey, on 22 June 1911. They commenced their visit to north Wales on 12 July at Holyhead, where they arrived from Dublin aboard the royal yacht *Victoria and Albert*. The investiture of Prince Edward as Prince of Wales took place at Caernarfon Castle on 13 July. The royal party returned overnight to the *Victoria and Albert* at Holyhead and on Friday 14 July undertook a visit to the University College of North Wales at Bangor, before continuing their journey via Afon-wen and Porthmadog to Machynlleth, where they were entertained over the week-end by the Marquis of Londonderry, at the Plas.

A visit to Aberystwyth took place on the Saturday, to lay commemorative stones at the site of the National Library of Wales and on Sunday, after a visit to Machynlleth parish church for the morning service, the day was spent at the Plas, presumably in relaxation before the following day's journey to Edinburgh, for a state visit to Scotland.

The LNWR commissioned photographs of the Royal Train at Caernarfon (sadly, not within the collection of the National Library), but the Cambrian Company appears to have overlooked the potential of such a prestigious occasion: at least, no official prints are known to survive and we are indebted to amateur cameramen for any record of these events on the Cambrian. The Royal Train left Machynlleth for Scotland at 10.00 a.m., in charge of Cambrian Railways 4–4–0s Nos. 81 (leading) and 83, and arrived at Whitchurch, where the LNWR again took over, at 12.10 p.m. The heavy ten-coach load of 321 tons had required the assistance of a third locomotive, banking at the rear, between Machynlleth and Talerddig.

Although he was present at Aber-miwl, Constable No. 19 must have gained only a very blurred impression of the Royal Train as it sped north on Monday 17 July, 1911.

[J. D. K. Lloyd.

36.

36. The photographer of the Royal Train at Aber-miwl also recorded the little branch train to Kerry (Ceri). Cambrian 0–6–0 No. 26, formerly *Ealswith* of the Lambourn Valley Railway, was purchased in 1904 and survived as GW No. 820 until it was purchased in 1931 by Mells Colliery near Frome, where it worked until scrapped in 1945. The composite carriage No. 84 was built in 1872 and scrapped when the Cambrian was taken over by the GWR in 1922; interestingly, this four-wheel carriage was permanently allocated to the Kerry service at this time, and was lettered accordingly.
1911.]   [J. D. K. Lloyd.

37. The joint Cambrian, Mid-Wales and Manchester & Milford station at Llanidloes *c.* 1900. The building's simple but elegant lines were never marred by the provision of a platform canopy, a factor which may have contributed to much sheltering in the doorways, resulting in marked discolouration of the stonework in these regions. Passenger services were withdrawn from Llanidloes at the end of December 1962; freight continued until 1967, but the grand old station survives as a listed building, now adjacent to the town's new bypass.
[DCH Coll.

38. The London North Western Railway platforms at Builth Road station, around the turn of the century. The Mid-Wales Railway platforms were located somewhat behind the camera, at a right angle to and beneath the LNWR tracks.
c. 1900.]   [DCH Coll.

39.

40.

42

39. Demolition of the Van branch of the Cambrian Railways, the last railway built by David Davies of Llandinam in 1870 originally for transporting lead ore from the Van mines, took place during March 1941. Rather ironically, one of the wagons in the demolition train was from Davies's south Wales venture — the Ocean collieries in the Rhondda. The locomotive was GW No. 819, formerly *Eadweade*, one of three Lambourn Valley engines purchased by the Cambrian in 1904; it was withdrawn in 1946.

[GC Coll.

40. Machynlleth station *c*. 1890 in a well-known image by John Thomas, which is included here as a fine example of his group arrangements, often assembled during the lunch hour when people could leave their work with the blessing of the management, and when the light was usually at its best. The pale-faced youth on the right of the buffer-beam, however, effectively obscures the identity of the engine which, unusually, sports no number on the cabside. Despite the inclusion of around thirty prospective customers on the plate, no original print is known to survive.

[JT Coll.

41. Old salts and landlubbers. Sailors, dockers and uniformed railwaymen assemble at Aberdyfi for John Thomas's camera. The group includes two figures somewhat out of keeping with the majority: the short, soft-hatted gentleman sporting a watch-chain, in the centre of the group, has something of the appearance of a doctor, whilst the hard-hatted figure nearby appears to be an official or owner. How many of the remainder, one wonders, sailed around the Horn?
c. 1885.]
[JT Coll.

42.

42. Built by Sharp Stewart & Co. at Manchester in 1864, 2–4–0 *Plynlimon* pauses during
    shunting operations on the foreshore at Aberdyfi, *c.* 1885. The gap in Bodfor Terrace,
    behind the locomotive, reveals the source of the slate rubble used as infill for the extension
    on the foreshore and wharf, completed by 1888.

[JT Coll.

43. The house built upon sand. Thomas Savin intended to ring Cardigan Bay with a series of
    grand hotels as logical destinations for thousands of early rail travellers. He anticipated a
    pattern popularized by British Rail's Golden Rail Holidays of the 1960s and 1970s by a
    century or more, but the ambitious scheme was ahead of its time. Although Savin built
    pilot hotels at Aberystwyth, Aberdyfi and Borth, they were never a great success. The
    Castle Hotel at Aberystwyth was quickly put up for sale in 1866, after little more than a
    year in use, but was not finally disposed of until 1872 when, at a fraction of its original cost,
    it became the nucleus of the University College of Wales. The Corbet Hotel at Aberdyfi
    survived a while longer, was occupied by Jesuits expelled from France in 1880 for a short
    period, but eventually became empty and was burned down in 1914.
        The most successful of the trio, shown here, was the Aberystwyth and Welsh Coast
    Hotels Company's Cambrian Hotel at Borth, photographed *c.* 1890. Later renamed the
    Grand, it survived as a hotel until the outbreak of the Second World War when it became
    a billet for HM Forces. In 1946, it was purchased by the Pantyfedwen Trust as a hostel for
    Urdd Gobaith Cymru, the Welsh League of Youth, but expensive running and mainten-
    ance costs caused the building's sale for re-development some twenty years later.

[JT Coll.

44. Plus-fours and portmanteaus — as commonplace in the pre-war railway station as
    clerestory-roofed coaches and steam locomotives. Passengers and railway staff at
    Aberystwyth load luggage aboard an east-bound train returning from the coast.
    c. 1930.]   [AJL Coll.

44

43.

44.

45.

45. Two 'Duke' Class 4–4–0s start an 'up' train from Aberystwyth, past concrete-posted bracket signals and the signal box. The old Cambrian engine shed stands on the extreme right and the locomotive shunting in the distance is either Cambrian 0–4–4T No. 10 or No. 19.
    c. 1930.]   [AJL Coll.

46. For two decades following the grouping of the railways in 1922, the Great Western brought considerable new investment to the Cambrian lines; the rebuilding of Aberystwyth station was a prime example. This exterior view, *c.* 1930, presents the station as the focal point of Aberystwyth transport, with an increase in road vehicles already apparent.

[AJL Coll.

4   THE NARROW GAUGE

Many regard the narrow-gauge lines as the most attractive aspect of railways in Wales although, almost unbelievably, there remain those who have yet to appreciate this enchantment. Admittedly, the little lines underwent great change when they ceased to serve the purpose for which they had been built and some would aver that their original charm has diminished and all but vanished.

The transportation of slate by rail finally ceased during the 1960s, with the closure of the Nantlle, Padarn and Penrhyn systems. The Glyn Valley Tramway had closed as early as 1935 and the Festiniog ceased in 1946. The Corris Railway survived until 1948 and the Talyllyn terminated its period in private hands with the death of its owner in 1950. That today's systems exist at all is a tribute to the almost endless man-hours and finance poured into them by enthusiasts who freely volunteer their time, skills and resources.

New developments of the last decade or so have seen the establishment of the narrow gauge in south Wales — at Henllan in west Wales and in the Brecon Beacons, where the Brecon Mountain Railway operates between Pant and Pontsticill. The latter line, particularly, can rival some of the more established systems of the north, for beautiful scenery is not confined to any one part of the Principality, but neither of the south Wales systems is represented in the National Library's archives.

The railway preservation movement was born in Birmingham in 1950 with the rescue of the Talyllyn Railway in distant Merioneth. This pioneer example has been emulated countless times and the Festiniog has also been miraculously resurrected to link Blaenau and Porthmadog once again by what must surely be the finest of all the little trains of Wales. Other survivors, the Welshpool & Llanfair line, the Fairbourne Railway, the emerging Welsh Highland Railway and the Vale of Rheidol — until recently, British Rail's only narrow-gauge, steam-operated line — have been joined by 'new' railways on old track-beds, principally the Padarn Lake Railway at Llanberis and the Bala Lake Railway, based at Llanuwchllyn.

If the railways of the 1990s frequently bear only a passing resemblance to the systems of fifty years ago, Wales is still fortunate it can offer thousands of summer tourists such a variety of survivors from its industrial past.

Narrow-gauge lines represented in this volume

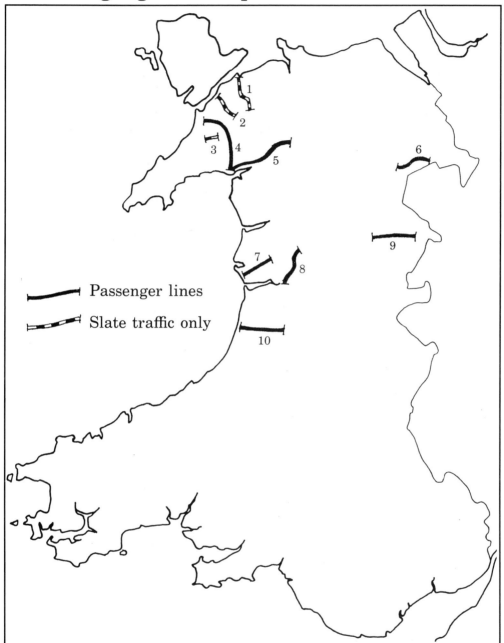

Key:
1. Penrhyn Railway.
2. Padarn Railway.
3. Nantlle Railway.
4. North Wales Narrow Gauge/
   Welsh Highland Railway.
5. Festiniog Railway.
6. Glyn Valley Tramway.
7. Tal-y-llyn Railway.
8. Corris Railway.
9. Welshpool & Llanfair Light Railway.
10. Vale of Rheidol Light Railway.

47.

48.

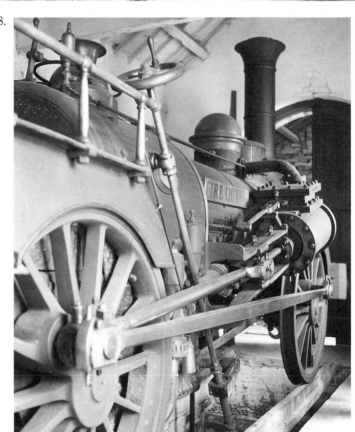

47. Part of the 3ft 6in.-gauge Nantlle Railway, typical of so many early tramroads throughout Wales, survived as a horse-tramway until its closure in *c.* 1960. This view shows a trainload of slates *en route* to Nantlle from the quarries.
    c. 1920.] [PPC.

48. The two major slate-only narrow-gauge lines in north Wales, however, were the 1ft 10¾ in.-gauge Penrhyn Railway and its more westerly neighbour, the Padarn Railway. This latter line, with a gauge of 4ft, was able to transport twin rows of the 1ft 10¾ in.-gauge wagons used in the quarries 'piggy-back' fashion, down to Port Dinorwic, where the dock-side lines again adopted the 1ft 10¾ in. gauge.

    None of the weird and wonderful steam-engines which took to the rails of Wales during the pioneer days were more bizarre than the Padarn Railway's two 4ft-gauge 0–4–0 tender engines, *Jenny Lind* and *Fire Queen*, built by A. Horlock & Co. of Northfleet Works, Kent, in 1848. The former was scrapped in 1886 but *Fire Queen* survived, bricked up in a shed at Llanberis, before being removed to the Penrhyn Castle Museum, Bangor, where it is now on public display. Geoff Charles overcame the difficult and cramped confines of the shed at Llanberis and produced this remarkable memento of *Fire Queen* at her resting-place of over eighty years. The unusual rail on which it stands, not unlike an enormous fire-bar, is also worthy of note.
    c. 1965.] [GC Coll.

49. The sidings at Port Dinorwic, unlike the Padarn Railway's main-line of 4ft gauge, reverted to the narrow gauge of the quarries, and were served only by a steep incline which burrowed beneath the A487 and the Bangor–Caernarfon railway line. The locomotives which shunted the quayside sidings were thus isolated from the remainder of the system for long periods and were stored in a small shed of their own. Here, No. 70, an Andrew Barclay 0–4–0WT, which spent all its working life at Port Dinorwic, trundles along the quay with two loaded wagons.
    c. 1956.] [GC Coll.

50. The locomotives of the nearby Penrhyn Quarries fell broadly into two main categories, both with the same narrow 1ft 10¾ in. gauge; small engines were confined to the internal quarry system and a few engines, somewhat larger in size, were responsible for haulage between Bethesda and Port Penrhyn, near Bangor.

The Geoff Charles Collection contains some memorable prints of both systems, three of which are reproduced here:
(I) Andrew Barclay 0–4–0WT *Cegin* represents those working at the lower quarry level. January 1959.]   [GC Coll.

51. (II) *Blanche*, one of the main-line engines, poses prettily on the quay at Port Penrhyn, whilst being coaled laboriously by its crew. Although the quay is almost deserted in comparison with previous years, a coaster, some oil-drums and both empty and loaded slate wagons serve to present Geoff Charles with what must rank as one of his finest railway images.
June 1961.]   [GC Coll.

52. (III) Chiaroscuro at Port Penrhyn is controlled in masterful fashion by Geoff Charles who encapsulated a momentary pause during what once was a routine procedure, the return of 'empties' along the main-line to the quarries.
June 1961.]   [GC Coll.

53.

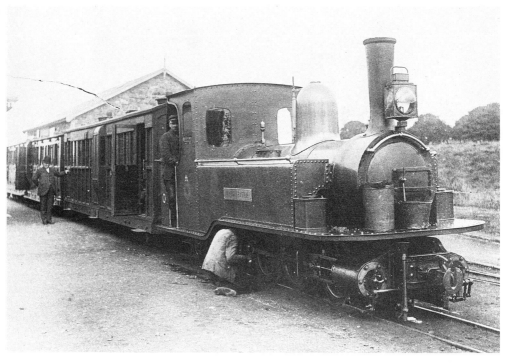

54.

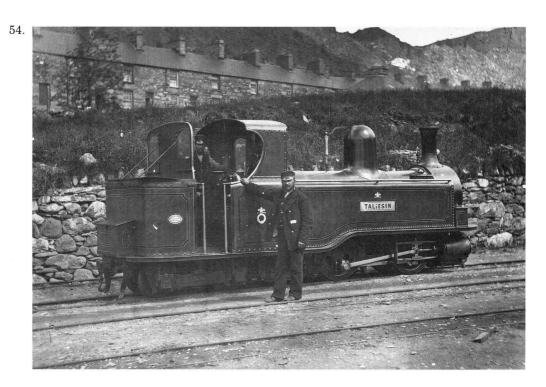

53. The North Wales Narrow Gauge Railway was opened in 1877 from Dinas Junction, on the LNWR Caernarfon–Afon-wen line, as far as a temporary station at the west end of Quellyn Lake in the heart of Snowdonia. The route on to Snowdon Ranger (later named Quellyn Lake) was open by 1 June 1878 and a further extension to South Snowdon (originally Rhyd-ddu) was in operation by May 1881.

    The initial services were worked by three interesting tank locomotives of the 0–6–4 wheel arrangement; *Moel Tryfan*, shown here, was built by the Vulcan Foundry in 1875, as was *Snowdon Ranger*, whilst *Beddgelert* was built by the Hunslet Engine Co. in 1877. *Beddgelert* was a conventional steam-engine, but both the Vulcans were single Fairlie types (*see next picture*).
    c. 1880.]   [MSA Coll.

54. 0–4–4T *Taliesin*, built by the Vulcan Foundry in 1876, and one of the Festiniog's most interesting locomotives, stands near Duffws station *c.* 1890. *Taliesin* was a single Fairlie type, that is, the cylinders were mounted on a bogie carried by the driving wheels, as opposed to the more normal practice of mounting on the rigid framework of the engine. The weight of the 20ft-long engine was thus supported by the swivelling power bogie and a smaller trailing bogie, permitting considerable flexibility on the Festiniog's tortuous track. Apparently, *Taliesin* was a speedy and economical machine which coped well with moderate loads and was frequently used on passenger and mail services. It survived until 1906 (when the name was transferred to a double Fairlie engine). The present Festiniog Company is currently planning the construction of a replica single Fairlie.

                                                                                   [JT Coll.

55. Surely one of the most familiar of early Festiniog images. Double Fairlie 0–4–0 + 0–4–0 *Merddin Emrys* stands at the line's northern passenger terminus at Duffws, with a long rake of quarry-workers' coaches.

    Some indication of the extent of the quarry workings may just be discernible in the hazy background; the Votty (*sic*) and Bowydd rope-worked incline rises steeply behind the rear of the train, whilst the railway's first double engine *Little Wonder* just creeps into the frame, extreme right.
    c. 1879/80.]   [JT Coll.

56.

57.

56. This view of Rhiwbryfdir, Blaenau Ffestiniog, shows the original trestle bridge of 1854
which carried the narrow-gauge Oakley Quarries lines across Afon Barlwyd and the later
standard-gauge LNWR branch from Llandudno Junction, which emerged from a two-mile
tunnel just beyond the bridge. The cottages lend some scale to the vast proportions of the
waste tips which, in one instance, slope directly to the rear of the properties. The quarry-
mens' zig-zag route to work and the adjacent incline for the slates are also noteworthy.
c. 1875.] [JT Coll.

57. Minffordd station, Festiniog Railway. An 'up' train, composed of four-wheel and bogie
stock, and headed by the double Fairlie engine *James Spooner*, waits for the photographer
to complete his work.
   The nearby Cambrian station is located just behind the camera position, at a right angle
to, and beneath, the Festiniog metals.
c. 1886.] [PPC.

58. Dôl-goch viaduct, Talyllyn Railway. The Talyllyn's original locomotive No. 1, *Talyllyn*,
and an 'up' train were recorded on Dôl-goch viaduct by the Newtown photographer John
Owen during the early years of the line's existence. This rare view of the open-cabbed No. 1
also reveals the brake-van with an open veranda.
   No. 1 was originally delivered from the Lowca Works of Messrs Fletcher and Jennings of
Whitehaven as an 0–4–0ST, but the long footplate overhang at the rear created problems
of stability. As a consequence, the line's second engine, No. 2 *Dolgoch*, which was still
under construction, was altered and given an extended wheelbase. No. 1 was then returned to Lowca in 1866/7 for modification to an 0–4–2ST, an alteration which had been
carried out by the time John Owen photographed it at Dôl-goch.
c. 1869/70.] [J. Owen, Newtown.

59.

60.

59. Talyllyn Railway train with engine No. 2 *Dolgoch*, at Abergynolwyn station, the passenger terminus of the line during the whole of its independent existence.
    c. 1920.]   [PPC.

60. The Talyllyn Railway's Travelling Booking Office, photographed at Abergynolwyn. The ticket-seller's window was constructed over the former open veranda.
    c. 1945.]   [PPC.

61. The nearby Corris Railway was built to the same, rather unusual, 2ft 3in. gauge as the Talyllyn; indeed, there were even proposals to link the two systems in 1907, but the scheme, and the prospect of Welsh narrow-gauge electric locomotives, came to nought.
    An Aberllefenni train here stands at Corris, comprising one of the railway's original saddle-tank engines built by the Hughes Engine Company, Loughborough, in 1878, and examples of the line's early bogie carriages, some of which were converted from the four-wheeled tramway coaches during the 1890s.
    c. 1900.]   [JT Coll.

62.

62. When the Corris Railway required a new engine to cope with an expected upsurge in the demand for slate after the First World War, the initial request was for a modern version of the line's original locomotives. By 1921, however, that design was no longer available as the manufacturer had been taken over by Kerr Stuart & Co., who produced their own design.

The new engine was delivered in 1921 and although numbered 4 on the Corris lists bore no evidence of that fact, only its maker's plate which declared it to be their No. 4047.

When the Great Western Railway purchased the line in 1930, it found it then had two Nos. 4047 on its books and so, presumably in order to prevent a *Star* from working up to Maespoeth, or the Kerr Stuart being rostered to a Paddington–Bristol express, the brass maker's plate was altered: 'No. 4047 1921' was removed (and stamped on the lower rim) and a steel figure 4 was fashioned and riveted in place.

Here, No. 4, as No. 4047, stands at Machynlleth on a Corris train, *c.* 1928.

[PPC.

63. The Welshpool & Llanfair Light Railway was also built to an unusual gauge for a Welsh railway, that of 2ft 6in. but unlike the other Welsh lines, its traffic was mainly agricultural. Here, Beyer Peacock 0–6–0T *Countess* pauses during a break in shunting at Llanfair Caereinion in April 1950. Fireman Fred Williams keeps company with John, the photographer's young son, whilst Ted Ffoulkes and M. L. Peate discuss the next move with the guard R. Morgan.

The clerestory van (right, background) is a former main-line vehicle grounded at Llanfair and used for the storage of perishable merchandise such as animal feed.

[GC Coll.

64. A pastoral view taken from the guard's van as 0–6–0T *Countess* traversed Powys, the 'paradise of Wales'*, *en route* to Llanfair Caereinion with coal, building materials and some mysterious sheeted merchandise.

*'Powys Paradwys Cymru' was the motto of the county of Montgomery.
April 1950.]   [GC Coll.

63.

64.

65.

65. 'Three little maids from school are we ...', all with eyes on *Countess* as she leads the
Llanfair train across the culverted Lledan Brook (beneath the timber baulks), past
Ballards Garage and toward Raven Square at Welshpool.
21 April 1950.]   [GC Coll.

66. The Glyn Valley Tramway used to run alongside the road between Chirk and Glynceiriog.
It was built to a gauge of 2ft 4½ in., for the purpose of conveying slate from the quarries to
the canal and the GWR main-line near Chirk. Here 0–4–2T *Dennis* and a mixed train
stand at Glynceiriog station. Note the locomotive wheels and motion discreetly obscured
by the metal skirt, as decreed by Board of Trade regulations governing locomotives
operating alongside public highways. The second carriage, an open third-class vehicle
built by the Midland Railway Carriage & Wagon Company in 1891, is also worthy of note
as it saw only limited use and was semi-retired at an early date.
c. 1900.]   [JT Coll.

67. Vale of Rheidol Railway No. 3 *Rheidol*, formerly Plynlimon & Hafan Railway *Talybont*,
was originally destined for Brazil when constructed in 1896, but the order was cancelled
and the little Bagnall 2–4–0T eventually spent most of its days between Aberystwyth and
Devil's Bridge. It was withdrawn by the GWR in 1924.
c. 1910.]   [AJL Coll.

68. Vale of Rheidol No. 3 *Rheidol*, sporting perhaps the world's best-dressed footplateman,
pilots one of the line's 2–6–2Ts up the final grades near Devil's Bridge.
c. 1911.]   [AJL Coll.

5   SOUTH-WEST WALES

Yet again, the need for a route to Ireland provided the primary reason for a line through Wales, although tramways and early railways had long been established in the Saundersfoot and Llanelli areas for the purpose of exporting the hinterland's high-quality anthracite.

As in north Wales, there were claims and counter-claims regarding the optimum port (such claims persist), but Fishguard eventually emerged as the most suitable contender as an outlet to southern Ireland, although it failed in its later bid to become a transatlantic port.

Apart from the main Irish connections to Neyland and Fishguard, the region's principal lines were the secondary railways constructed between Pembroke, Tenby and Whitland, and the lines north from Carmarthen. The most prominent of the latter was the Carmarthen & Cardigan Railway, initially built as a broad-gauge line. It was followed by the later Manchester & Milford Railway which eventually ran from Aberystwyth to Pencader, where running powers were granted over the re-gauged Cardigan line to Carmarthen. David Davies of Llandinam played a leading role in the construction of both the Pembroke & Tenby and the Manchester & Milford lines. In due course, both entered the Great Western fold; the P & TR in 1897 and the M & MR in 1911.

Of the remainder, only three need mention here; the railways of north Pembrokeshire which sought an alternative route to Fishguard, the deceptively titled Taf Vale Railway which ran from Whitland to Cardigan and, finally, the branch from Llandeilo to Abergwili Junction near Carmarthen. This was originally part of the Llanelly Dock and Railway system but came under the control of the LNWR in 1871. The remaining west Wales lines became the property of the GWR — the Whitland to Cardigan line in 1890 and the North Pembrokeshire & Fishguard Railway in 1898.

The main Fishguard line remains open to passenger traffic today, as do the branches from Clarbeston Road to Milford Haven and Whitland to Pembroke. It is also worth noting that the Central Wales service from Swansea to Shrewsbury makes use of the Llanelli–Pontarddulais route, since closure of the original line from Pontarddulais to Swansea (Victoria), via Gowerton and Killay, in 1964. The remaining lines fell to the Beeching axe during the 1960s.

South-West Wales

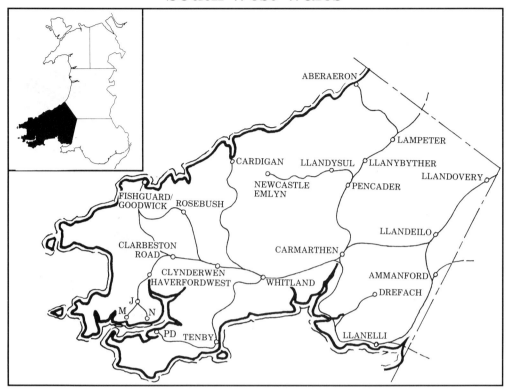

Key: J – Johnston
     M – Milford Haven
     N – Neyland
     PD – Pembroke Dock

69. Before Fishguard became the main south Wales port for the Irish service, the broad-gauge South Wales Railway saw New Milford, or Neyland as it was later known, as the most convenient port for the Irish service. This view depicts some of the later facilities at Neyland.
c. 1914.] [PPC.

70. The GWR station at Fishguard has been much photographed over the years, particularly around 1909 when Cunard's *Mauretania* used to call on transatlantic sailings. Despite the GWR's efforts and the running of special trains to Paddington, the rival claims, first of Liverpool then of Southampton, ensured the transatlantic venture at Fishguard was but short-lived.
c. 1920.] [PPC.

69.

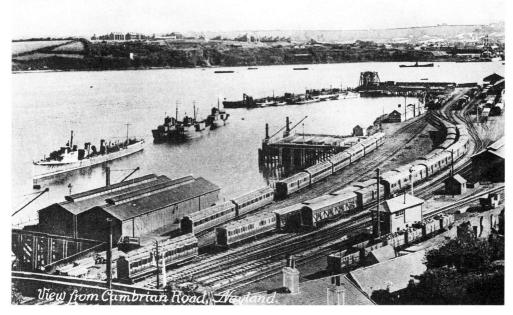

View from Cambrian Road, Neyland.

70.

FISHGUARD HARBOUR STATION

71.

72.

ABERAYRON STATION.

71. The title of the North Pembrokeshire Railway is conveniently used here to embrace three small companies, the Narberth Road & Maenclochog Railway, the Rosebush & Fishguard Railway, as well as the North Pembrokeshire & Fishguard Railway itself; they provided an alternative route from Clynderwen to Fishguard, coveted at one time by the London & North Western Railway. Very few photographs exist of the Maenclochog Railway but this view of Rosebush shows the small station, engine shed and a short train.
   c. 1890.]   [JT Coll.

72. A favourite amongst the rural byways of west Wales was the branch from the M & MR at Lampeter to Aberaeron, the last portion of which, from the creamery at Felin-fach, survived until 1973. Here, a former Bristol & Exeter Railway carriage, as GW No. 6479, was in use as an inspection saloon at Aberaeron, around the time the branch was opened in 1911. The locomotive was the Wolverhampton-built 0–4–2T No. 840.

                                                                                                 [PPC.

73. The Manchester & Milford Railway appeared to be a classic example of how not to promote a railway for it served neither town in its title but had to be content to offer a moderate service from Aberystwyth, through the heart of rural Cardiganshire, to Pencader.
   M & MR No. 2 *Carmarthen* is depicted at Carmarthen. Built by Sharp Stewart in 1866, No. 2 later acquired this rather strange, Stroudleyesque cab. Its career came to an abrupt end when the boiler exploded at Maesycrugiau in 1890; miraculously, both driver and fireman escaped unhurt.
   c. 1880.]   [WDJ Coll.

74.

74. New Quay Road, latterly known as Bryn Teifi, apparently boasted a full-height platform from the outset, in marked contrast with many small stations in rural areas where low platforms were much in evidence — one or two persist on the Cambrian Coast line (see also picture 77).

   This charming line-up of Cardiganshire characters seems unperturbed at the non-appearance of an M & M train and is obviously happy to entertain, and be entertained by, the photographer.
   c. 1880.]   [JT Coll.

75. As a result of the Regulations of Railways Act 1889, all railway companies were obliged to complete improvements to their signalling arrangements. Previously, signals, and the interlocking of signals and points, were often basic and the application of safety procedures lacked consistency.

   Signal boxes were found at only the more important locations; elsewhere, the signal and point levers were frequently out in the open and devoid of shelter. This small cabin was being erected at Tregaron.
   c. 1890.]   [TWJ Coll.

76. Perhaps the M & M's most intriguing locomotive was the Crewe-built 2–4–0 purchased in 1891 and sold for £150 in 1900: it features prominently in this well-known station group by John Thomas. Most interestingly, the glass-plate negative for this image was not amongst those acquired by the NLW from Sir Ifan ab Owen Edwards, but the original print is undoubtedly Thomas's work, although he is seldom credited. This photograph's survival in print form only makes one regret anew that the vast bulk of Thomas's work has been 'lost': what other gems were discarded, one wonders?
   c. 1895.]   [JT Coll.

77. Llandeilo station, originally on the Vale of Towy Railway, before the station was rebuilt and the protruding 'wing' with clock removed as it restricted the platform width. Apart from the later addition of a new canopy, this building is little altered — even the low platform survives in 1990, but there is now a distinct possibility that it may be remodelled once more, to create space for a projected Llandeilo bypass.

    The wooden portion, comprising the unusual signal-box and attendant signal, has long since disappeared; even the more modern brick-built box on this site is now boarded up and out of use. A Pembroke & Tenby Railway timetable, on the 'up' platform, is just discernible on the original print.
    c. 1880.]   [JT Coll.

78. Carmarthen Valley Junction signal-box was located to the south of Llandeilo, where the GWR branch to Carmarthen left the Shrewsbury–Swansea LNWR line. The 'T' and 'S' discs suspended outside the box were an indication — in pre-telephone days — that assistance was requested from telegraph or signal repair-men.

    The box closed in the 1950s, and one of its last operators was in 1990 still employed by British Rail at Llandeilo.
    c. 1900.]   [DCH Coll.

79. Llanelli station, with a Churchward 4–4–0 on a Fishguard express. Several '*Flower*' Class locomotives were stationed at Fishguard in the period preceding the First World War.
    c. 1910.]   [PPC.

80.

Train at Oystermouth Station

80. The Mumbles Railway, opened in 1807, was operated along the shores of Swansea Bay, between Swansea and Mumbles, and was the first passenger-carrying railway in the world. Short-sighted policies, however, contributed to its demise and eventual closure as recently as 1960. It is not difficult to imagine the attraction of such a train just thirty years later.
   c. 1905.]   [PPC.

6 SOUTH-EAST WALES

The railway network of south-east Wales eventually evolved as one of the most complex in Britain. By the outbreak of the First World War there was hardly a valley within the region without at least one rail service, whilst in many instances rival companies were to be found operating on opposite sides of the valley, and confluence or other strategic points frequently saw three or even four rival companies jostling for favoured locations in order to secure a share of the heavy and lucrative traffic.

The earliest fully fledged rail system, as opposed to the pioneering tramroads, was the Taff Vale Railway which, in 1840, had emerged rapidly on the heels of the Llanelly Railway & Dock Company (1839) to the west. The Taff Vale was opened from the new Bute Dock at Cardiff to Abercynon, and within a year extended through to Merthyr Tydfil. Elsewhere in the region, the established tramways held sway for some years but, inevitably, the recently built Taff Vale quickly demonstrated the advantages of new locomotives and trackwork, and tramways such as the Duffryn Llynfi & Porthcawl Tramroad and the more easterly Rumney Tramroad felt compelled to adapt and modernize, although the new railways did not emerge for a further ten to fifteen years, mainly because of financial difficulties.

Foremost amongst the early systems which complemented the Taff Vale were the Rhymney Railway and the Monmouthshire Railway & Canal Company, whilst the rival Great Western Railway and London North Western Railway either promoted or purchased lines in an attempt to secure some of the market. The Newport, Abergavenny & Hereford Railway (together with that company's later Taff Vale Extension) and the Merthyr, Tredegar & Abergavenny Railway are prime examples of attempts by the English-based companies to penetrate the coalfield and ease the traffic towards the major markets beyond the Severn.

Other notable companies in this region were the Brecon & Merthyr and the Neath & Brecon Railways. Later companies were frequently born out of the chronic congestion and extreme frustration which accompanied the development of the coalfield toward the end of the nineteenth century. Prominent amongst these may be listed the Rhondda & Swansea Bay Railway and the Port Talbot Railway but, undoubtedly, the major scheme at this time was David Davies's Barry Dock & Railway Company, stoutly engineered to cope with vast tonnages of export coal for a century and beyond, but whose peak period of operation barely survived two decades.

The coal trade reached its zenith in 1913; thereafter affected by war and depression it began a decline which was accelerated by increased use of the internal combustion engine, and conversion of the world's navies from coal to oil-burning. The timely grouping of Britain's railways into the four main groups in 1922/3 facilitated the closure of those lines which were becoming uneconomic to operate or which doubled up on facilities better offered by an adjacent line. Often, the most recent lines to be constructed were amongst the earliest to be closed.

The Great Western Railway headed the group which was granted responsibility for most of the south Wales lines; it derived enormous benefit from the amalgamation and finally gained control of most of the routes and docks in the area which it had coveted jealously for so many years. The only lines of importance outside its control were the former London & North Western and the Midland Railways in south Wales; these became part of the new London, Midland & Scottish Railway and comprised the Central Wales line from Craven Arms to Swansea, Hereford to Swansea (via Brecon) and Abergavenny to Merthyr (with some running powers via the old Rhymney line to Cardiff).

Nationalization of Britain's railways in 1948 failed to unite the railway systems of south Wales; this only evolved in 1963, with a redrafting of the regional boundaries which had previously adhered closely to the old companies.

81.

South-East Wales

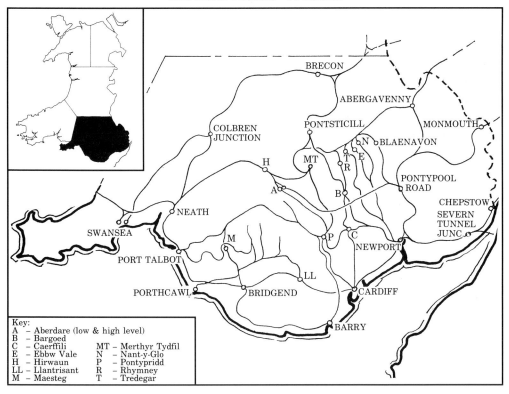

Key:
A – Aberdare (low & high level)
B – Bargoed
C – Caerffili   MT – Merthyr Tydfil
E – Ebbw Vale   N – Nant-y-Glo
H – Hirwaun   P – Pontypridd
LL – Llantrisant   R – Rhymney
M – Maesteg   T – Tredegar

81. Pont-rhyd-y-cyff Viaduct *c.* 1898, when newly built to carry the Port Talbot Railway across the Darran valley and over a tramway and the sidings of the Llynfi Valley Colliery. The locomotive on the lower level appears to be an ancient contractor's engine; that accompanying the brake-van on the viaduct had, at this early date, to be one of two engines of this type on the PTR, either No. 3 or No. 15. Both were built in 1897, being withdrawn in 1930 and 1929 respectively. A sister engine (No. 26) survives as GW No. 813, on the Severn Valley Railway in Shropshire.

[PTD & R Coll.

77

82.

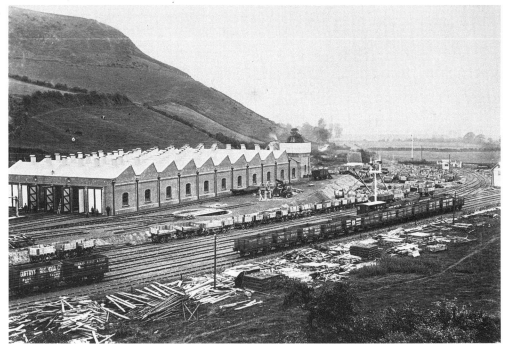

83.

82. The six-road Duffryn locomotive shed under construction on the Port Talbot Railway in 1898. The small, light-coloured spoil wagons used by the contractors are prominent in the centre and right distance, whilst private-owner colliery wagons occupy the foreground, bearing the names of Harman, Nurse & Son, Llanelly; Oliver H. Thomas, Neath; the Llynfi Colliery; T. P. Thomas & Co., Cardiff; Pyman Watson & Co., Oriental, Merthyr & Cardiff; the Bryn Colliery, Duffryn Rhondda Co., Port Talbot; and North's Navigation, Bridgend. 1898.] [PTD & R Coll.

83. A ballast train run by S. Pearson & Son, the contractors on the new Port Talbot Railway line, works up the grade from Pontyrhyll Junction in 1898.

[PTD & R Coll.

84. A Port Talbot Railway train of empty wagons returns from the docks, past the immaculate station at Maesteg in 1898.

[PTD & R Coll.

85.

85. The platforms of passenger stations were usually very low, or non-existent, during the early years, but as the railways developed many of the more primitive stations were rebuilt. The Taff Vale Railway instigated a fairly extensive programme of renewal at the turn of the century and, in the example illustrated, the presence of the photographer has caused all work to come to a halt during rebuilding of the platforms at Aberaman, near Aberdare, *c.* 1905.

[WDJ Coll.

86. The topography of Wales decreed that the easier routes lay either along the coastal strips
or, inland, along the valley floor. The earlier companies obviously secured the prime routes
and late developers, epitomized by the Barry Railway (1889–1922), had little option but to
indulge in extensive tunnelling and the construction of costly viaducts. The greatest of the
latter was undoubtedly the viaduct at Llanbradach, which was 2,400ft long, 125ft high,
and constructed in 1904. When the Barry was acquired by the GWR in 1922, as a result of
the grouping, Llanbradach viaduct was deemed surplus to requirements and was subse-
quently demolished by the Royal Engineers in 1936.
c. 1930.]   [WDJ Coll.

87.

88.

87. Penrhos Junction (I) looking east. Apart from a local service between Pontypridd, Caerffili and Newport, Penrhos Junction (virtually across the main road from the later British Aircraft Corporation engine-testing plant at Nantgarw) was not a location normally frequented by passenger trains. In pre-grouping days, no fewer than three separate companies passed through the narrow defile; the Alexandra Docks & Railway Company and the Rhymney Railway crossed each other on the level in the middle distance, whilst the Barry Railway crossed both, as depicted in the following photograph. The last tracks at this site were lifted in 1984, but the three-arch bridge, carrying a minor road, still survives.
   c. 1935.] [WDJ Coll.

88. Penrhos Junction (II) looking west. A 56xx 0–6–2T labours up the 'big hill' from Taff's Well on the former Rhymney Railway main-line to Cardiff (before the opening of the direct route via Caerffili Tunnel). The connecting line to the Barry Railway's yard at Penrhos is on the left; the AD & R line to Pontypridd is on the right, whilst the Barry main-line, to connect with the Llanbradach viaduct and the upper Rhymney valley, crosses by means of the girder bridge.
   Until three prints were discovered at the NLW of this 56xx-hauled train, no photographs of the complete Barry viaduct at Penrhos were thought to exist. The steel girders were removed in 1936; the brick piers remain.
   c. 1935.] [WDJ Coll.

89. The operation of heavy trains over steeply graded inclines gave rise to many spectacular accidents over the years. The great majority were not photographed but W. D. Johns was able to record two such incidents. This photograph portrays a runaway which piled into the stop-block at Taff's Well, at the foot of the steep gradient from Aber Junction, known locally as 'the big hill'. The locomotive was GW 2–6–2T No. 5195.
   c. 1940.] [WDJ Coll.

90.

90. Another incident also involved a runaway, on the Rhymney main-line at Llanishen. The train was obviously diverted into a stop-block to prevent an even greater disaster had it been allowed to career further down the incline to Cardiff Queen Street station. The engine of the runaway train, a Taff Vale A Class 0–6–2T, is almost obscured by the mound of crushed Tredegar wagons and spilled coal.
July 1936.]   [WDJ Coll.

91. Snow-bound on the Brecon & Merthyr Tydfil Junction Railway. Further hazards were presented by adverse weather, well illustrated by the scene near Pontsticill on the line to Pant and Dowlais Top, when severe conditions prevented the two pannier tank engines from making further progress. No further information accompanies the original print but, judging by its angle, the first locomotive appears to be derailed.
c. 1940.]   [WDJ Coll.

92. Subsidence, usually the result of coal-mining, frequently affected the valley lines of south Wales. Some locations were persistent trouble-spots; subsidence could also occur elsewhere with little or no warning. The location of this particular occurrence, in a rural part of south Wales, has not been identified.
c. 1940.]   [WDJ Coll.

91.

92.

93.

93. Work on the track is frequently thought to be amongst the least glamorous of railway operations. Here, the gauge and clearances are checked near the Pontypridd, Caerphilly & Newport Junction, just south of Pontypridd.
c. 1939.]   [WDJ Coll.

94. Nowadays, pre-assembled panels and pointwork are used to renew track; in former years, most new track was assembled 'on site', as in this instance where the fang bolts are being tightened near PC & N Junction, Pontypridd.
   c. 1939.]   [WDJ Coll.

95.

95. The fireman sits atop the boiler of a former GW 52xx 2–8–0T at Aberbeeg as he replenishes the water supply during the 'down' working of fuel for one of the coal-burning power stations located near the coast. This traffic has dwindled in a dramatic manner. Cheaply produced foreign coal is now frequently imported through the very docks at Barry which were constructed a century ago for the export of Welsh steam coal. Coal exports reached a record figure in 1913 when over 11 million tons left Wales through Barry alone.
c. 1955.]   [GC Coll.

SUGGESTIONS FOR FURTHER READING

ANDERSEN, V. R., and FOX, G. K., *An Historical Survey of the Chester to Holyhead Railway* (Oxford Publishing Co., 1984).

BARRIE, D. S. M., *The Barry Railway* (Oakwood Press, 1962).

——, *The Brecon and Merthyr Railway* (Oakwood Press, 1957).

——, *Regional History of the Railways of Great Britain, Vol. 12, South Wales* (David & Charles, 1980).

——, *The Rhymney Railway* (Oakwood Press, 1952).

——, *The Taff Vale Railway* (Oakwood Press, 1939).

BAUGHAN, P., *Regional History of the Railways of Great Britain, Vol. 11, North and Mid Wales* (David & Charles, 1980).

BOYD, J. I. C., *The Festiniog Railway* (2 vols., Oakwood Press, 1956, 1959).

——, *Narrow Gauge Railways in Mid Wales* (2nd ed., Oakwood Press, 1970, 1986).

——, *The Tal-y-llyn Railway* (Wild Swan, 1988).

BRIWNANT-JONES, G., *Railway through Talerddig* (Gomer, 1990).

CHRISTIANSEN, R., *Forgotten Railways: North and Mid Wales* (David & Charles, 1976).

——, *Forgotten Railways: Severn Valley and the Welsh Borders* (David & Charles, 1988).

—— and MILLER, R. W., *The Cambrian Railways* (2 vols., David & Charles, 1967, 1968).

COZENS, L., *Mawddwy, Van and Kerry Railways* (Oakwood Press, 1972).

GABB, G., *The Life and Times of the Swansea and Mumbles Railway* (D. Brown & Sons, 1987).

GREEN, C. C., *Cambrian Railways Album* (2 vols., Ian Allan, 1977, 1981).

——, *North Wales Branch Line Album* (Ian Allen, 1983).

——, *The Vale of Rheidol Light Railway* (Wild Swan, 1986).

HOLDEN, J. S., *The Manchester and Milford Railway* (Oakwood Press, 1979).

KIDNER, R. W., *The Cambrian Railways* (Oakwood Press, 1954).

——, *The Mid Wales Railway* (Oakwood Press, 1990).

KNEALE, E. N., *North Wales Steam* (2 vols., Oxford Publishing Co., 1980, 1986).

LEE, C. E., *The Swansea and Mumbles Railway* (Oakwood Press, 1988).

MILNER, W. J., *The Glyn Valley Tramway* (Oxford Publishing Co., 1984).

MORGAN, H., *South Wales Branch Lines* (Ian Allan, 1984).

MORRIS, J. P., *North Pembroke and Fishguard Railways* (Oakwood Press, 1969).

MOUNTFORD, E. R., *The Cardiff Railway* (Oakwood Press, 1987).

OWEN-JONES, E. S., *Railways of Wales* (National Museum of Wales, 1981).

PAGE, J., *Forgotten Railways: South Wales* (David & Charles, 1979, 1988).

—, *Rails in the Valleys* (David & Charles, 1989).

POPPLEWELL, L., *A Gazetteer of the Railway Contractors and Engineers of Wales and the Borders 1830–1914* (Melledgen Press, 1984).

PRICE, M. R. C., *The Pembroke and Tenby Railway* (Oakwood Press, 1986).

—, *The Saundersfoot Railway* (Oakwood Press, 1964, 1989)

—, *The Whitland and Cardigan Railway* (Oakwood Press, 1976).

REAR, W. G., *LMS Branchlines in North Wales* (Wild Swan, 1986).

TASKER, W. W., *The Merthyr, Tredegar and Abergavenny Railway* (Oxford Publishing Co., 1986).

WILLIAMS, H., *Davies the Ocean* (University of Wales Press, 1991).